MW00981242

610.28   Arnold, Nick.
ARN   Medicine: now and into the
          future /

TOMORROW'S TECHNOLOGY

MEDICINE
NOW AND INTO THE FUTURE

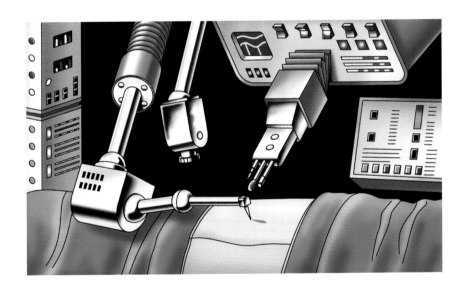

Nick Arnold

ILLUSTRATED BY INDUSTRIAL ART STUDIO

Thameside Press

U.S. publication copyright © Thameside Press 1999

International copyright reserved in all countries.
No part of this book may be reproduced in any
form without written permission from the publisher.

Distributed in the United States by
Smart Apple Media
123 South Broad Street
Mankato
Minnesota 56001

Produced for Thameside Press by Bender Richardson White
Project editor Lionel Bender
Designer Ben White
Text editor Sue Nicholson
Illustrations by Industrial Art Studio
Consultants Steve Parker and Virginia Whitby
Picture researchers Cathy Stastny, Jane Martin and
Daniela Marceddu
Page make-up Michael Weintroub
Project Production Kim Richardson

Printed in Singapore

ISBN 1-929298-39-0
Library of Congress Catalog Card Number: 99-71371

Photo credits
Custom Medical Stock Photo, Inc., Chicago: 6 (Copyright
1991 David Weinstein & Associates), 8-9 (Copyright
1991 J. L. Carson), 11tr (Copyright 1991 DCRT/
NIH/CMSP),11b (Copyright 1991 J. L. Carson),
12 (Copyright 1992 Amethyst), 16 (Copyright 1998
Eric Herzog), 22r (Copyright 1991 Michael English,
M.D.), 25 (Copyright 1996 C.M.S.P.), 27 (Copyright
1994 John Meyer).
Science Photo Library, London: 13 (National Cancer
Institute), 24 (Peter Menzel), 26-27 Alex Bartel).
Rainbow Photos, Housatonic, MA: 4l (Larry Mulvehill), 4-5,
5, and 11tl (all by Dan McCoy), 14 (Will McCoy),
14-15 (Rosenfeld Images Ltd.), front cover and
17 (Dan McCoy), 18 (Dan McCoy, James Sullivan),
19 (Dan McCoy/ Medtronic Inc.), 20, 22l, and 29
(all by Dan McCoy), 28-29 (Hank Morgan).

Words in **bold** appear in the glossary on pages 30-31.

CONTENTS

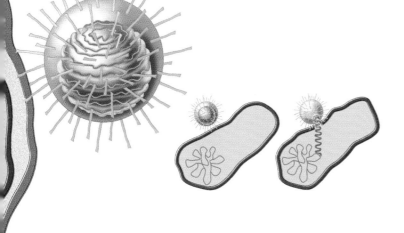

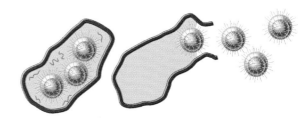

INTRODUCTION

Do you remember the last time you were ill? You probably felt terrible at the time, but the chances are that the illness got better on its own—perhaps after a few days off school. But some diseases are far more serious and, if they are not treated properly, they can even kill. People who suffer from these diseases or who have been seriously injured need medical help to stay alive.

WHAT IS MEDICINE?

Medicine is the science that aims to find out what disease you are suffering from and to help you recover your strength and health. The word medicine also means any drug that helps to treat or cure an illness, or any operation by a surgeon. People who are trained in medicine spend many years learning how the body works, how and why it becomes ill, and how best to treat it.

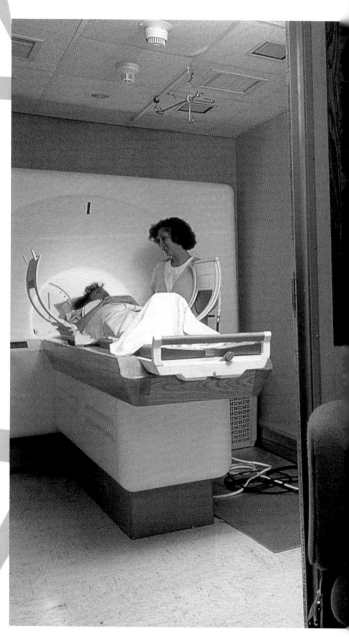

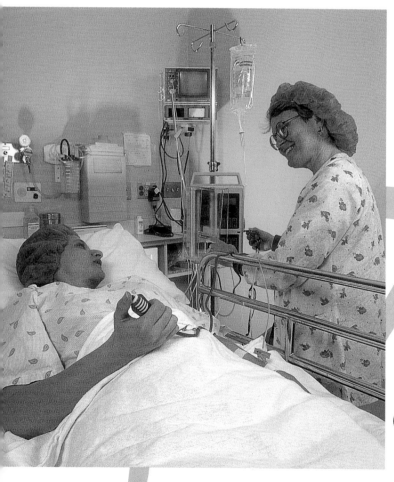

A patient wakes up after an operation. During the operation, an **anesthetic** drug makes the patient unconscious and blocks pain.

This patient is being given an MRI (magnetic resonance imaging) scan. Harmless radio waves are directed at the patient's body, which is placed in a magnetic field. Different parts of the body absorb the radio waves by varying amounts, and this shows up on a computer screen.

A CHANGING SCIENCE

Medicine is changing all the time. A hundred years ago, medical treatments such as **x-rays**, **transplants**, and blood **transfusions** were little known. Today they are commonplace and the technology of medicine is developing faster than ever before. Computers, scanners, and monitors are a part of everyday medicine.

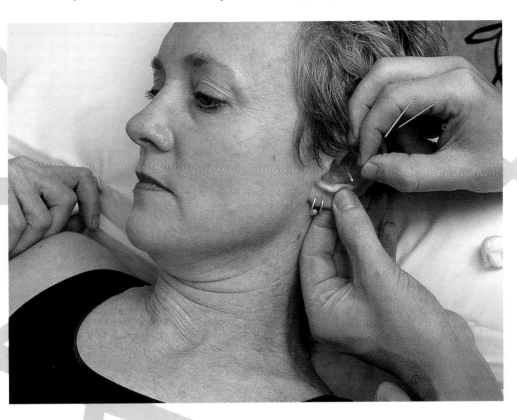

ALL SORTS OF THERAPIES

Although western medicine relies on drugs and surgical operations to treat disease, there are alternative or complementary treatments available, such as **acupuncture**, **hypnosis**, or **chiropractic** techniques. They can all ease pain, although scientists are not sure how they work. Today, these treatments are increasingly available in hospitals and health centers.

Acupuncture needles have been inserted into this patient's ear to relieve tension or pain. The needles are placed in parts of the body that are connected in some way to the site of the pain or disorder.

▶ FUTURE TREND

Predicting the future is very difficult. A new invention may be in daily use in five years' time, or it may be delayed for 30 years. It may never happen at all. What is certain is that technology develops all the time. *Future Trend* looks at new developments, which may happen in 20, 40, or even 60 years. They may seem impossible to us today, but for people 60 years ago, so were heart transplants.

MEDICINE AND DISEASE

For as long as humans have suffered from disease and ill health, other people have been trying to heal them. The first doctors were found in many parts of the ancient world, including China, Egypt, and the Middle East. An ancient Greek doctor named Hippocrates of Cos (460–370 B.C.) is usually credited with giving healing a more scientific basis. His practical approach to medicine earned him the title "Father of Medicine." He was skilled at treating disease and also recognized that the body can recover from some illnesses without treatment.

MEDICINE TODAY

Modern medical care is organized in two main stages. Primary care is provided by your family doctor. Like Hippocrates, the doctor makes a **diagnosis** of the illness. He or she may then write a **prescription** for the medicine you need to take to get better. If the illness is serious or further tests are needed, the doctor refers you to another doctor who is an expert in that disease. This is known as secondary care, and might involve a stay in hospital. Here you will be looked after by nurses and possibly operated on by trained surgeons.

A delicious salad is rich in vitamins and fiber, which are essential for maintaining good health.

MAKING A DIAGNOSIS

- The doctor asks about the patient's past health (in case an old illness has flared up).

- The patient describes their **symptoms** to the doctor.

- An examination of the patient pinpoints the cause of the symptoms

▶ FUTURE TREND

ALL SPACED OUT?
Living in space can cause space sickness and long-term damage to the body. Bones and muscles can waste away in conditions of **zero gravity**, because they are not properly exercised. As space travel becomes more common, scientists may develop drugs to ease the effects of weightlessness. In the future, space medicine may become as important as ordinary medicine.

TODAY'S MAJOR ILLNESSES

Disease often results from an attack on the body by germs (see page 12). There are many germs known to doctors that can cause disease. Some major illnesses, however, are not caused by germs, but by problems in a particular part of the body. These might result from weakness because of old age, or they could be brought on by an unhealthy lifestyle.

HIPPOCRATES

Unlike previous doctors, Hippocrates did not think that disease could be cured by gods or magic. Instead, he noted his patients' symptoms and examined them to make a diagnosis. If necessary, he then prescribed simple drugs and other treatments to help his patients get better.

MAJOR ILLNESSES

Brain

▶ Strokes may be caused by blood clots in the brain. **Cells** in the brain become starved of **oxygen** normally carried in the blood. Strokes can result in **paralysis** and blindness.

Heart

◀ Heart attacks are caused by fatty deposits blocking the **arteries** that feed blood to the heart muscle. The muscle stops working properly. Death can follow if the heart fails to pump life-giving blood and oxygen to the rest of the body.

Plaster cast over broken bone

Stomach and intestines

◀ Cancers can affect any part of the body. They are caused by cells that divide uncontrollably until they form a lump known as a tumor.

▶ Road accidents are a major cause of death among people up to the age of 40. Victims often suffer broken bones, but the injuries can be much more serious if they involve damage to the brain or the internal **organs**.

Joint

◀ Arthritis affects the joints between bones, resulting in stiffness and pain in movement. Arthritis may result from an infection by germs, or from long-term damage to the joint caused by overuse.

UNHEALTHY LIFESTYLES

An unhealthy lifestyle can contribute to disease:

▶ Smoking increases the risk of heart attacks, lung cancer, and many other lung diseases.

▶ Taking certain illegal drugs can lead to addiction—a craving for the drug. Many have other dangerous side effects too.

▶ Heavy drinking of alcohol can cause addiction and damages the liver.

▶ Lack of exercise and overeating can make a person seriously overweight. This puts an extra strain on the lungs, heart, bones, joints, and many other body parts.

▶ Not brushing teeth allows germs to build up. The germs make acid that causes **tooth decay**.

THE SECRET OF GENES

Some illnesses are not caused by germs or an unhealthy lifestyle. They are programmed into the body by genes. Genes are complex chemical codes carried on tiny structures called chromosomes. There are 46 chromosomes in every cell of the body. Genes control the way each cell grows and develops and, in this way, shape your overall appearance.

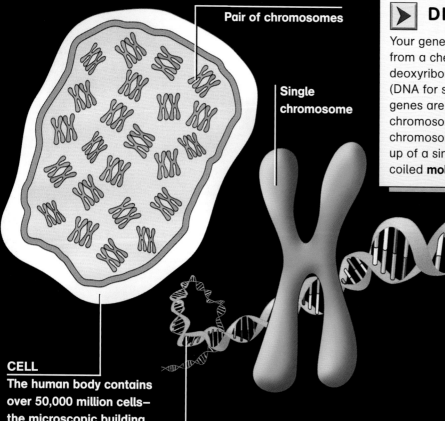

Pair of chromosomes

Single chromosome

▶ DNA

Your genes are made from a chemical called deoxyribonucleic acid (DNA for short). The genes are stored in chromosomes. Each chromosome is made up of a single, tightly coiled **molecule** of DNA.

CELL
The human body contains over 50,000 million cells—the microscopic building blocks of all living things.

Twisted strand of DNA

GENETIC DISEASES

The chromosomes in just one cell contain 6 feet of DNA and over 100,000 genes. Every time a cell divides, the DNA in that cell copies itself. A mistake in the copying process could trigger one of about 4,000 genetic diseases. These diseases could be passed on to future generations in the DNA contained in **sperm** or eggs. One example is cystic fibrosis, a group of lung diseases caused by certain base pairs missing from a particular gene. Fortunately, DNA copies itself very accurately and genetic diseases are rare.

BASE PAIR
A gene consists of pairs of chemicals (base pairs). The four chemicals in DNA are adenine, guanine, cytosine, and thymine. Base pairs are organized like the rungs of a twisted ladder.

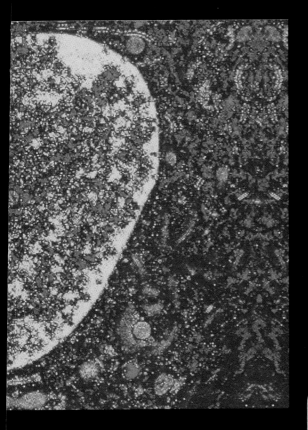

Chromosomes are found in the central area of a cell known as the nucleus. This photograph shows the nucleus of a body cell, magnified 10,000 times.

GENE MAPPING

In 1988, scientists launched the Human Genome Project—a study designed to map every gene in the human body. Mapping a gene is hard work. Scientists have to find which chromosome the gene is on, then record the exact order of its tens of thousands of base pairs. However, by 1997, the sites of 450 diseases had been found on just one chromosome. And the scientists had made a key discovery—a gene that seems to control whether tumors develop (see page 10).

GENE SCREENING

Chemical tests for DNA are called gene screening. Results are read by a computer that can spot a range of genetic diseases. Many people are critical of DNA testing, even though it is vital in detecting certain diseases. Some people are afraid of DNA testing because it might show that they have a disease that cannot be cured.

▶ FUTURE TREND

CODED SECRETS?

Since your DNA code is unique to you, it could be used for identity cards. Your DNA codes could be kept on police files or included in cash cards to help you get cash from the bank. But should people like the police or big companies know your DNA code? If your code showed up a genetic disease, you might find it harder to get life insurance, buy a home, or find a job.

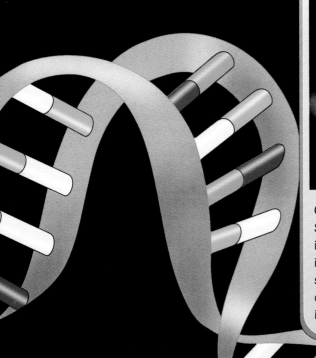

GENE THERAPY

In 1990, scientists at the National Institutes of Health, in the U.S.A., added a human gene to a **virus**. Viruses are tiny living things that cause illnesses such as colds and influenza. The genetically altered virus was injected into the body of a cancer patient. Incredibly, the virus attacked and killed the tumor cells, because the added human gene was one that orders cells to die. This thrilling discovery makes possible a cure for some kinds of cancer, but it is only one form of gene therapy.

HOW A VIRUS WORKS

Influenza virus

Host cell

A virus breaks into a living cell and hijacks its DNA to make copies of itself. The influenza virus, shown here, mainly attacks the nose and throat. It is particularly common in winter.

LIVING MESSENGERS

Scientists use a technique called gene splicing to alter the DNA of a virus. The DNA is spliced, or cut, using a chemical called an **enzyme**. Then a length of human DNA including the desired gene is added to the viral DNA. The DNA of the virus is also altered so that it will not multiply inside the body and make the patient sick.

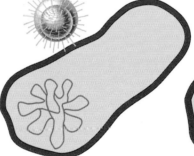

1 The surface of a cell has receptors that recognize and take in chemicals that the cell needs.

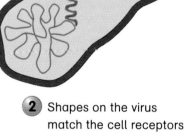

2 Shapes on the virus match the cell receptors. The cell allows the virus's DNA inside.

▶ FUTURE TREND

GERMS TO FIGHT GERMS?
Genetically altered viruses could be programmed to boost the body's defense system against disease. Scientists have found certain viruses that attack germs called **bacteria**. In the future these viruses, known as bacteriophages, could be used to destroy harmful bacteria.

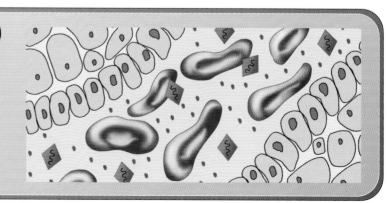

BINDING DNA

Scientists are developing drugs that may one day prevent genetic diseases. They work by binding to the DNA in miscopied genes. The drugs stop the DNA from making more copies of itself—so, when the miscopied genes die out, they are not replaced.

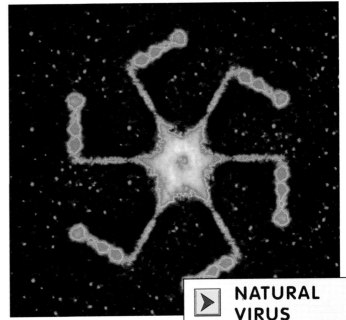

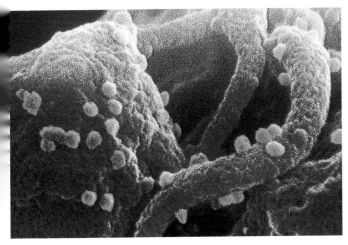

Viruses (colored green) attack a white blood cell. They appear tiny in comparison to their victim.

3 The virus uses the cell's DNA to make more copies of itself.

4 New viruses burst from the worn-out cell.

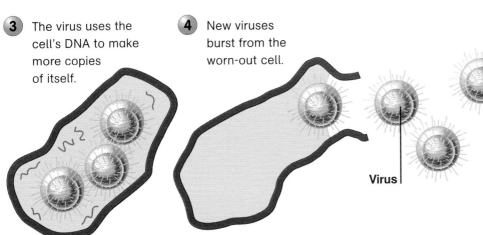

Virus

▶ NATURAL VIRUS

The bacteriophage virus above is one of a naturally occurring group of viruses that attack the bacteria that cause disease in humans. The six projecting points are **proteins**. They can recognize sites on the bacterial cell where the virus can inject its DNA, leaving its protein outer shell on the surface of the cell. The viral DNA forces its victim to make new copies of the virus.

Viruses break away from an infected white blood cell. The cell is now dead and the viruses will seek out another cell to attack. Millions of cells can die before the patient even starts to feel unwell.

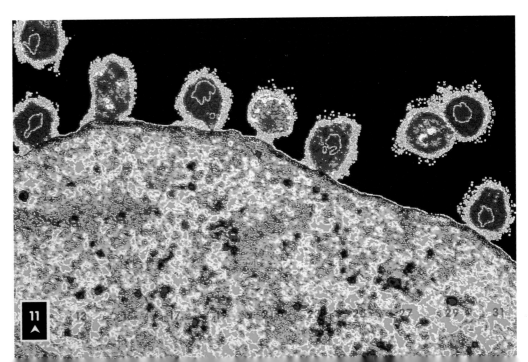

THE WAR AGAINST GERMS

 Germs include bacteria, viruses, and tiny organisms called **protozoa**. They can get into the body through droplets of water from the breath of a sick person, in food that hasn't been cooked properly, by direct contact, through dirty water, or via insect bites or transfusions.

THE IMMUNE SYSTEM

Your body is equipped with an army of germ-fighters—white blood cells. T-cells and B-cells are two types of white blood cell. T-cells round up germs and destroy dead cells. B-cells produce germ-killing chemicals called **antibodies**. Once white blood cells have defeated an illness, they keep a record of the germs they destroyed. This allows them to make the right antibodies if the same germs reappear. That is why you are **immune** once you have had an illness such as chickenpox, and are unlikely to catch it again.

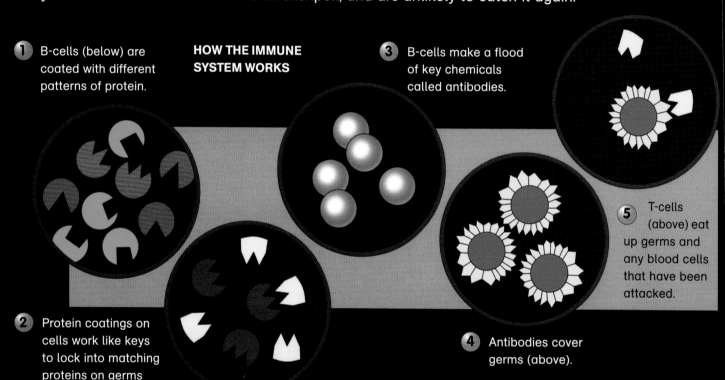

HOW THE IMMUNE SYSTEM WORKS

1 B-cells (below) are coated with different patterns of protein.

2 Protein coatings on cells work like keys to lock into matching proteins on germs (right).

3 B-cells make a flood of key chemicals called antibodies.

4 Antibodies cover germs (above).

5 T-cells (above) eat up germs and any blood cells that have been attacked.

▶ The most common method of vaccination is by an injection.

VACCINES TO THE RESCUE

A vaccine is an injection of dead germs, or the chemicals that they make. The body's immune system destroys the dead germs easily and will attack the living germs the next time they get into the body. In the future, vaccines could be made from harmless viruses with added genes to give them the same chemicals on their outer coats as more dangerous viruses.

FUTURE TREND

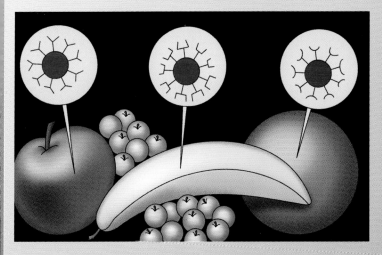

HEALTHY FRUIT?

In the future, scientists could breed genetically altered fruit containing antibodies. We could eat the antibodies as part of our normal diet—perhaps without even realizing what we are doing. One day, we may no longer need to have injections—we could enjoy a delicious antibody fruit salad instead!

THE GERMS FIGHT BACK

When germs copy their genetic material, they make more mistakes than human cells. This kind of error is called a **mutation** and it may result in new kinds of germs. This is why people can catch a new kind, or strain, of influenza every year. Some new germs, such as new strains of the lung disease tuberculosis, cannot be killed by existing drugs. These types of germ are said to be "drug-resistant." Scientists have to alter the chemistry of the drugs so that they kill the new breeds of germs.

 A scientist squirts special red gel into a dish. She is growing bacteria for a research project—the gel will provide food for the germs. Viruses cannot be grown in this way, because they need living cells in order to multiply.

THE AIDS VIRUS

AIDS is caused by a virus called HIV which attacks a type of T-cell. Ultimately, the virus wrecks the immune system, leaving the victim helpless against the attacks of other germs. By 1999, over 40 million people worldwide had been infected by the AIDS virus. Of these, 14 million people had died of AIDS. But these figures are estimates and the true picture could be even worse. Most drugs used to treat the AIDS virus are designed to stop the virus from copying itself.

SMART DRUGS

New drugs are constantly being developed. One range is made from chemically altered antibodies designed to attack a particular disease. Other drugs may carry chemical switches that alert T-cells to attack a target germ. Some of these powerful new drugs of the future are being designed on computer screens.

DRUGS ON SCREEN

Using computer-aided drug design (CADD), scientists display a model of a target protein in the body, then match up drug molecules to see whether these can join onto the protein. Next, they make and test the drug in the form that works best. Testing can take many years because no drug is allowed to be used on people unless it has been shown to be as safe as possible.

This pharmacist in Peru, South America, sells drugs made from plants taken from the Amazon rain forest. Scientists estimate that of all the different plants and animals on Earth, 40 percent are found in the rain forests.

▶ FUTURE TREND

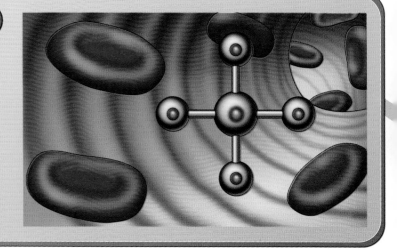

MINIATURE MESSENGERS?
In the future, drugs could be carried to where they are needed inside our bodies by tiny **nanorobots.** The nanorobots could be programmed to obey spoken commands. The dosage of the drug could also be varied by voice instructions —or even by brain wave patterns! One day there may be drugs for every imaginable condition, including fat-destroying drugs that would help people who are seriously overweight.

Drugs that can be swallowed are made as pills or capsules, or with sugar coating. Capsules and sugar coating break down and release the drug in the body's digestive system. Every day, people in western countries swallow tens of millions of drugs as part of medical treatment or to relieve pain.

▶ DRUG DOSE

Drugs must he delivered in the right amounts. One way to do this is to encase the drug in a substance called a **polymer**. The polymer breaks down slowly and harmlessly inside the body. This makes the drug escape slowly in the right dosage.

Polymer capsule

Drug

GENETICALLY ENGINEERED DRUGS

People who suffer from **diabetes** may need insulin—a **hormone** that controls the levels of sugar in their blood. Insulin can now be produced by genetically altered bacteria in large steel vats called bioreactors. Animals can also be used to make genetically engineered drugs. Scottish scientists have bred a sheep with an added human gene. The sheep produces milk containing a protein vital for the human liver and lungs.

NATURAL MEDICINES

Many lifesaving drugs are found naturally, in plants. Scientists can add the plant gene that makes the substance to the DNA of an animal or a bacteria cell to produce the drug. For example, cyclosporin-A blocks the immune system and stops the body's defenses from attacking transplanted organs. The drug was originally found in a Norwegian mushroom but is now made by genetically altered bacteria.

▶ SHARE OF THE PROFITS?

Global drugs companies are constantly searching tropical rain forests for plants that can be used to make medicines. But native peoples and governments of the rain forest countries are now claiming a share in the drug profits because the genes are taken from their local plants.

THE INSIDE STORY

Some injuries or illnesses do not show on the outside of the body even though they are serious and can be life-threatening. This is why scientists are developing new techniques that give an ever-clearer picture of our insides.

This surgeon is using an endoscope to examine a patient. The surgeon's clothes, mask, and gloves are designed to stop germs from entering the patient's body.

ENDOSCOPES

An endoscope is usually a flexible tube, small enough to be inserted into one of the body's natural openings or through a small cut called an incision. Air blown down the tube pushes the organs aside and gives the doctor a good view of the area that needs examining. Other endoscopes have tiny tweezerlike forceps that can grab a sample of the diseased area for further testing. Endoscopes are also used in surgery (see page 18).

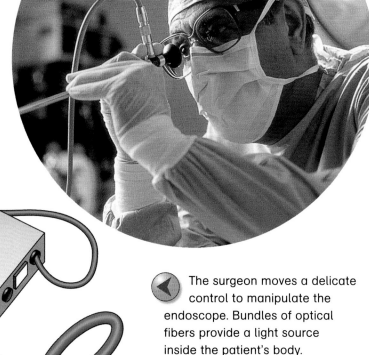

HOW AN ENDOSCOPE WORKS

The surgeon moves a delicate control to manipulate the endoscope. Bundles of optical fibers provide a light source inside the patient's body.

Control arm

Air is forced down this tube

Tube inserted into patient's body

Forceps

ULTRASOUND SCANNERS

Ultrasound scanners bounce high-pitched sounds off organs in the body and record the echoes. A computer uses the echoes to build up a moving image of the body part being examined. This could be a heart valve or a baby in the womb. Regular ultrasound scans are used to check the development of an unborn baby as it grows.

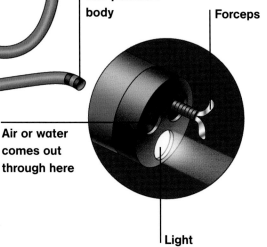

Air or water comes out through here

Light

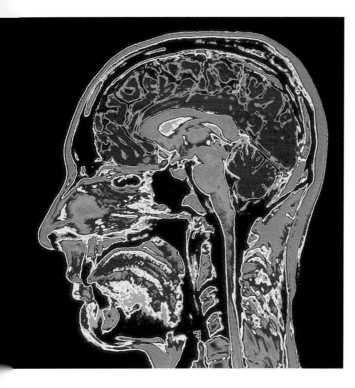

X-RAY AND MRI SCANNERS

CT (computerized tomography) scanners use a beam of very weak x-rays that moves around the body. The x-rays produce an image of the inside of the body from different angles. MRI places the patient in a magnetic field, then uses bursts of radio waves to build up a picture of tissue—and even flowing blood. The images produced by both CT and MRI are interpreted by a computer which creates a television picture.

This MRI scan of a patient's head clearly shows the brain. MRI can provide moving images of organs such as the brain and the heart.

HOW AN MRI SCANNER WORKS

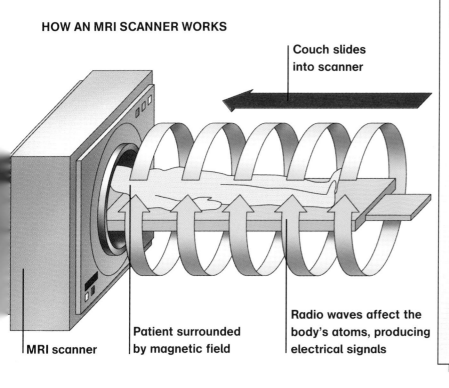

Couch slides into scanner

MRI scanner

Patient surrounded by magnetic field

Radio waves affect the body's atoms, producing electrical signals

▶ AN MRI SCAN

- The patient lies on a couch.

- **Electromagnets** produce a magnetic field.

- Curved panels contain coils that produce radio waves. The radio waves make the central cores of **atoms** in the body spin, producing radio or electromagnetic signals.

- Signals from the atoms are picked up in the coils.

- A computer makes the signals into an image, filtering out unwanted signals from body fat and muscles.

▶ FUTURE TREND

SCANNING FOR SICKNESS?
One day, your doctor might examine you with a handheld scanner, which might look a bit like a television remote control. The doctor would pass the scanner over your body, and the machine would provide a complete readout of your state of health and any illnesses you may have.

FRONTIERS OF SURGERY

Traditional surgery meant cutting open the patient, but modern surgeons can reduce damage to the patient's body by using keyhole surgery and inserting an endoscope. The surgeon then performs the operation using tiny forceps, scissors, or even a **laser** mounted on the endoscope. The surgeon sees what he or she is doing on a television picture relayed from the same or a second endoscope.

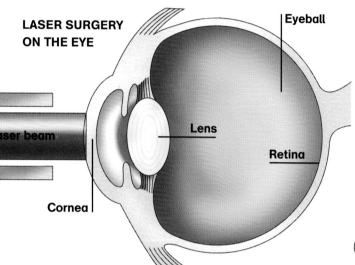

LASER SURGERY ON THE EYE

Eyeball

Laser beam

Lens

Retina

Cornea

LASER SURGERY

In recent years, lasers have replaced scalpels for some intricate cutting work. One advantage is that heat from the laser beam seals the ends of small blood vessels so that the patient loses less blood than in an ordinary operation. Lasers can be precisely controlled. This is very useful in delicate surgery, such as eye operations.

A laser burns a small amount off the cornea, to help the lens focus light more clearly on the retina.

▶ FUTURE TREND

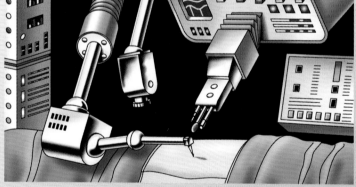

ROBO CHOP?
One day, operations could be performed by robots, although experienced surgeons would still be needed to supervise their work. Robot surgeons could be programmed to operate with pinpoint precision. This would be especially useful in brain surgery, where mistakes can have fatal results. The surgeon could control the robot by using a computer and a virtual reality (VR) headset. Imaging devices linked to VR simulators already help surgeons to practice before the operation.

▶ NEW BLOOD

If a patient loses blood during an operation, they may need a transfusion. Every year, more and more transfusions are performed, causing a worldwide shortage of blood. At the end of the 1990s, artificial blood came into use. This is made up of substances called perfluorocarbons that carry oxygen through the body just like real blood.

The color of these red blood cells (seen through a microscope) is due to a chemical pigment that carries the atoms of oxygen needed by cells to stay alive.

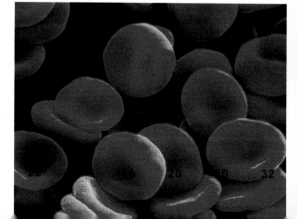

SOUND CURE

An ultrasound machine can produce sound waves far too high for the human ear to detect. These are used to create images of the body (see page 16), but also to blast away unwanted kidney **stones**. Kidney stones are buildups of salts and other minerals in the kidney. The ultrasound machine aims the sound waves directly at the kidney stone. The sound waves cause **vibrations**. This makes the kidney stone vibrate, until it shakes itself to pieces.

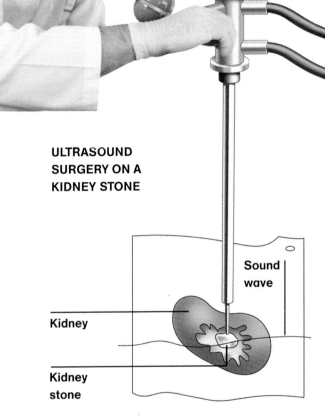

Ultrasound machine

ULTRASOUND SURGERY ON A KIDNEY STONE

Sound wave

Kidney

Kidney stone

BRAIN BLAST

Brain tumors can be zapped in a similar way, with **gamma rays** fired from outside the head. The gamma knife transmits 201 beams of gamma rays toward the tumor, all from different angles. The treatment is painless and does not damage the rest of the brain.

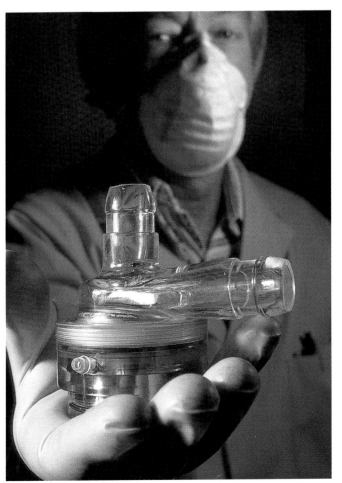

HELPING THE HEART

The heart has four chambers for pumping blood. It also has valves to control the flow of blood. If these fail, the results can be fatal. Surgeons can fit artificial valves and silicon rubber implants to assist or even replace valves or chambers. The implant is placed alongside the patient's own heart and powered from outside the body. Another approach is to **graft** muscles from the shoulder onto one of the arteries leading from the heart. An electronic device called a **pacemaker** makes the muscle squeeze in time with the heart's own beating and boosts the heart's pumping power.

 This surgeon is holding an artificial heart valve.

If parts of the body become diseased, they may be replaced by transplants or artificial implants. In 1954, surgeons in Boston, Massachusetts, successfully transplanted a kidney. In 1967, South African surgeon Christiaan Barnard carried out the first heart transplant. The patient died after 18 days. Today, transplants of the heart, lung, kidney, and liver are fairly routine. Patients are treated with drugs that stop the immune system from attacking the transplanted organ.

TISSUE TRANSPLANTS

Tissue transplants are the least complex transplants to perform. For example, skin grafts are given to people who are badly wounded or burned. Surgeons often use skin taken from elsewhere on the patient's body so that the graft is not rejected. Tissue is also fairly easy to store, as it can be successfully frozen until it is needed.

SPARE PARTS

As the demand for new body parts grows, scientists have had to find alternatives to parts from human donors. Artificial implants are made from special metals or plastics that the immune system does not attack. They are commonly used to replace hips, arms, or legs. Artificial limbs are now so advanced that they can be wired up to undamaged muscles that can twitch in response to signals from the brain. In turn, these muscles control the movement of the limb.

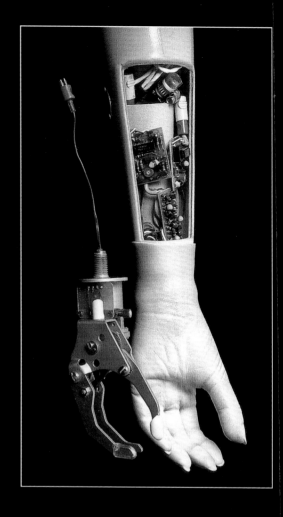

An artificial arm developed by the University of Utah, U.S.A. The arm works by making tiny electrical impulses produced by the muscles of the upper arm more powerful. The wearer can use these signals to move their artificial arm.

▶ FUTURE TREND

LIVING ROBOTS?

In the future, it may be possible to replace every part of the body, including the brain, with transplants or artificial implants. It might even become possible to create living robots that are made entirely from implants and human body parts. But this would pose some tricky questions. For example, should a living robot have the same rights as a human being?

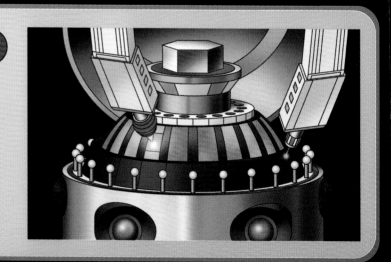

GROWING NEW ORGANS

Another possibility that scientists are exploring is growing transplant organs. In the 1990s, scientists bred genetically altered pigs whose organs can be used in transplant surgery. A human gene added to the organs makes a protein that stops the human immune system from attacking the transplant. Pig heart valves have been used to replace damaged human ones and pig skin grafts have treated burn victims. But is this technology cruel to the pigs? If so, should it be banned even if it saves human lives? In the longer term, scientists are hoping to get round this problem by growing organs from cells taken from fertilized human eggs or cultures of human cells that are grown in the laboratory.

Brain is still human

Skull plate to repair broken skull

Artificial eye linked to brain (see page 25)

Cochlea implant hearing aid linked to brain

Electronic voice box

Artificial shoulder

Mechanical heart valve

Mechanical heart pump

Artificial blood

Artificial kidney filters blood

Artificial stomach

Artificial knuckle

Artificial artery

Electrodes along spine produce nerve signals to move muscles

Artificial hip

Metal femur (thighbone)

Artificial knee

▶ TRANSPLANTS OF THE FUTURE

Surgeons are learning how to replace more and more parts of the body with implants and transplanted organs. At the same time, scientists are devising new methods to preserve transplant organs. The organs could be specially dried and treated with chemicals, allowing them to be frozen without damaging the living cells that make them up. This means that the organs can be easily stored and transported to wherever they are required.

Metal bones

Artificial foot

A BIONIC PERSON OF THE FUTURE?

PROBING THE BRAIN

The brain is vital in controlling the body's key functions. The most amazing area is the wrinkly region covering the top of the brain. This is the highly folded cerebral cortex with its billions of interconnected nerve cells. The cortex makes you conscious of the world around you and produces your personality, thoughts, and memories. Only now, are scientists beginning to discover how it works.

MAPPING THE BRAIN

The brain has about a thousand different zones and each has a specific job. As you look at this page, some areas of your brain are helping you view your surroundings while others allow you to focus on the area you are reading. Your memory and language-processing centers allow you to understand the words. Scientists can map how the brain works because blood flowing into the active areas of the brain shows up on MRI scans.

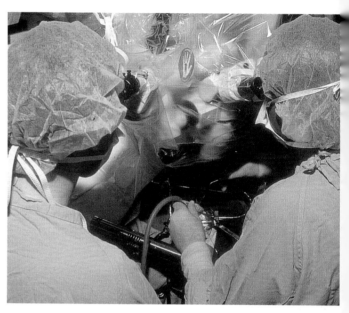

These surgeons are performing delicate surgery on the brain. The covers keep germs from getting into the exposed brain, and the microscopes help the surgeons to make out tiny details as they work.

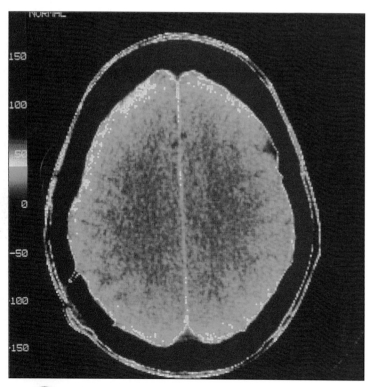

 A CT scan of a patient's head shows resistance to x-rays as colors. The dense material of the skull with high resistance to x-rays is shown in red. The more watery brain appears green.

▶ BRAIN WAVES

The brain produces waves of electrical activity, called brain waves. Brain waves can be detected by and monitored on an electroencephalograph (EEG) machine.

THE POWER OF BRAIN WAVES

People who are disabled or have damaged brains can control machines using their brain waves. At present, these do simple jobs, such as turning lights or televisions on or off. In the future it may be possible for people who cannot talk to use their brain waves to control an electronic **larynx** and produce speech.

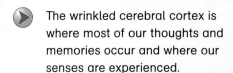 **INSIDE THE BRAIN**

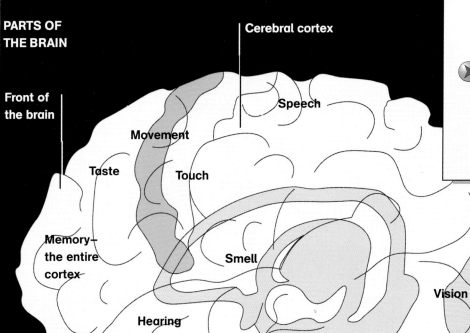

PARTS OF THE BRAIN

- Cerebral cortex
- Front of the brain
- Speech
- Movement
- Taste
- Touch
- Memory— the entire cortex
- Smell
- Hearing
- Vision
- Back of the brain
- Digestion and breathing
- Cerebellum

The wrinkled cerebral cortex is where most of our thoughts and memories occur and where our senses are experienced.

The lower and middle regions of the brain are concerned with controlling body functions, such as digestion and breathing.

The rounded cerebellum at the base and rear of the brain coordinates movements and stores the memory of physical skills, such as riding a bike.

▶ FUTURE TREND

BIONIC BRAINS?

In the future, scientists could build artificial brains. There are already computers that recognize speech and human faces. These could help people with sick or damaged brains remember their friends and family. Artificial memory implants could be used to boost the power of healthy brains. Another possibility would be to link a machine rather like a VCR to the brain, which would then display a person's thoughts and dreams on a screen.

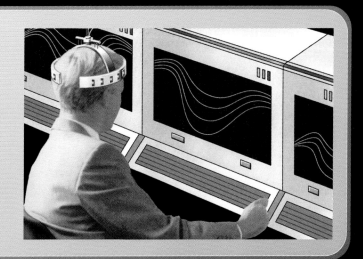

LIVING WITH DISABILITIES

The nervous system (right) is a complicated network of nerves linked up to the brain. It gives us information about what is going on around us and allows us to interact with other people. One of the biggest challenges facing surgeons is to help people whose nervous systems do not work properly—perhaps as the result of an accident, or because a genetic disease caused them to be born that way.

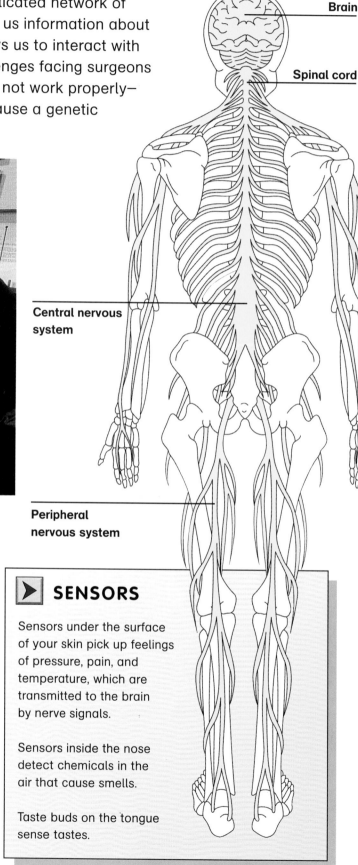

Brain

Spinal cord

Central nervous system

Peripheral nervous system

A man uses a microphone to control his computer by voice. Specially adapted computers like this one help disabled people to communicate.

YOUR VITAL SENSES

Your body senses what is going on around it through your senses of vision, hearing, touch, taste, and smell. Each sense depends on a different sense organ—the eye, ear, skin, tongue, or nose. These five sense organs have one feature in common: they all turn information received from outside the body into tiny nerve signals that pass to the brain. The brain then processes the nerve signals received from the senses and you see, hear, feel, taste, and smell.

SENSORS

Sensors under the surface of your skin pick up feelings of pressure, pain, and temperature, which are transmitted to the brain by nerve signals.

Sensors inside the nose detect chemicals in the air that cause smells.

Taste buds on the tongue sense tastes.

SOLVING THE SYMPTOMS

Traditional aids for the disabled gave people more independence but did not cure the disability. Guide dogs help the blind to get around, for example, but not to see for themselves. Wheelchairs transport paralyzed people, but do not enable them to walk.

REBUILDING NERVES

Today, scientists are devising exciting new techniques to rebuild damaged senses. Some paralyzed people cannot move because their nerves no longer transmit signals from their brains. Damaged spinal nerves do not normally regrow. But it is now possible to implant electrodes along the backbone which send signals to a person's nerves and make their limbs move. Surgeons are also developing ways to transplant healthy nerves to replace the damaged ones. Other researchers are testing drugs that could help damaged nerves to regrow and reconnect with each other.

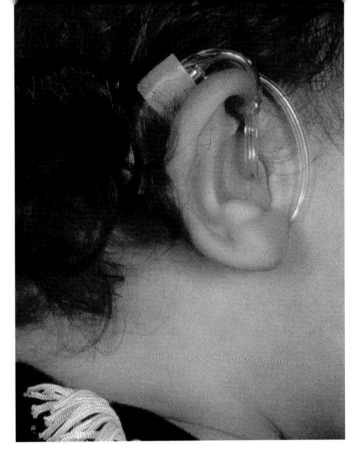

 This child is wearing a hearing aid. The device uses microelectronic circuits to amplify sound waves (make them more powerful), so the wearer can hear the sounds.

SILICON VISION

Scientists are developing artificial retinas that use light-sensitive **silicon chips**. The chips turn light into electrical signals. These are transmitted to the nerves using tiny electrodes under 0.08 inch long, enclosed in a glass sheath. As this technology develops, the pictures blind people see in their brains will become clearer and more detailed.

ARTIFICIAL HEARING

In one form of deafness, tiny hairs inside the cochlea—a fluid-filled coiled structure in the inner ear—are damaged. If they are working properly, the hairs in the cochlea pick up sound vibrations and turn them into nerve impulses. A cochlea implant is a device that uses electrodes instead of hairs to send impulses to the hearing centers of the brain.

▶ FUTURE TREND

SUPERSENSES?
In the future, people might extend their senses using a new machine. They could wear headsets that allow them to hear higher and lower sounds than our ears can make out. The device could also allow people to see infrared and ultraviolet light. (These are types of light that the human eye cannot pick up.) It might even give them a magnetic sense, to allow them to navigate better.

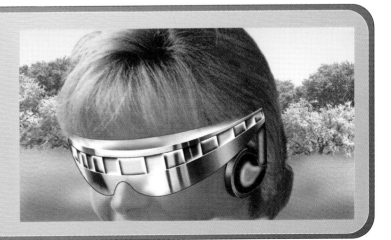

DESIGNER BABIES

By studying DNA, doctors can test an **embryo** for genetic diseases and, if necessary, gene therapy can alter the genes. In the future, gene therapy may also allow parents to choose whether their baby is a boy or a girl, whether it will be athletic or not, and many other characteristics. Will this prove to be a good thing?

TEST-TUBE BABIES

Some women cannot have babies because of blockages in the fallopian tubes that lead to their ovaries. In these cases it is possible to remove eggs from the woman's ovary and fertilize them with sperm. Children conceived in this way are sometimes described as "test-tube babies" (although test tubes are not actually involved). The developing eggs are placed in the woman's womb. If a fertilized egg is not needed it can be frozen in liquid **nitrogen** (a chemical treatment followed by rapid freezing, which stops any large crystals of ice forming that could damage the egg).

A woman's ovaries release a pinhead-sized egg every month. The egg was made before the woman was born, and stored in her ovaries. As well as DNA, it contains a food supply to provide the energy to begin dividing if it is fertilized.

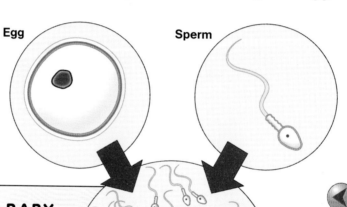

Egg **Sperm**

A man can make about 100 million sperm a day—that is about 1,100 every second! Each sperm is just 0.002 inch long. It swims by beating its whiplike tail from side to side.

Conception–sperm joins with egg

Division of cells

▶ FROM EGG TO BABY

Every baby starts off as an egg produced by its mother and a sperm made by its father. Each of these contain 23 of the 46 DNA-carrying chromosomes required to make a new human being.

The egg is stored in the ovaries. The egg travels to the womb via a fallopian tube.

The sperm joins with the egg. The two sets of DNA come together.

The egg divides to make two cells. Each cell contains all 46 chromosomes. The cells continue to divide for nine months, building a complete, new baby.

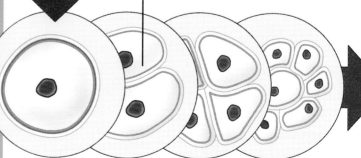

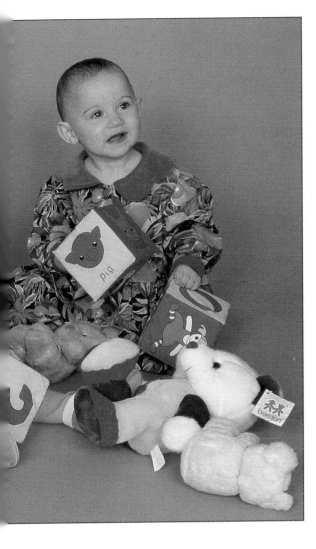

PROGRAMMED FOR LIFE?
In the future, unborn babies could be genetically altered. They might be given genes that destroy cancer cells but do not normally become active. If the child grew up and developed a tumor, an injection of a drug would activate the gene. The tumor would then die and the person would remain healthy.

◀ Identical twins are real-life clones—they have the same DNA. This happens because the fertilized egg split in two, and each half developed into a baby.

CLONING HUMANS

A clone is a living thing with the same DNA as another. Since the clone has the same genes, it looks exactly the same as the animal that the DNA came from. In 1997, researchers at Roslin, Scotland, announced the birth of a cloned sheep called Dolly. To create Dolly, the scientists used a cell containing DNA from a ewe, and an egg cell from another sheep from which the DNA had already been removed. A tiny electric shock encouraged the two cells to merge and then start dividing to make Dolly. In the future, this technique might even be used to clone humans. One day, a woman could give birth to a child who is an exact copy of her when she was a baby—or even of someone else.

▲ Sperm can be stored for long periods at extremely low temperatures.

CAUSE FOR CONCERN?

Advances in genetic technology worry many people. Should parents choose what their children will be like? Genes influence intelligence and temper—so how would you feel if your parents had chosen what you were like even before you were born? Should people have the right to clone themselves?

A HEALTHY FUTURE?

In the future, people will live far longer and there will be more people on Earth than ever before. Does this spell a healthy future? Or will the new breakthroughs in medicine only result in new problems?

A GROWING POPULATION

Because people are living longer, and more and more babies are being born, there are more people in the population. In many poorer countries, large families are common. This means more mouths to feed and more people for doctors to treat. There may also be more overcrowding and more chances for disease to spread. In the future, healthcare may have to be shared—rich people who were living longer and already enjoying good healthcare would pay to help poor people who were at risk from disease. This could be done through a world health tax.

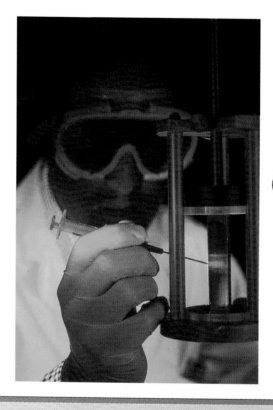

This virtual reality (VR) headset gives the wearer a three-dimensional (3D) image of the structure of the heart and the interior of the chest. In future, doctors may wear such headsets to control robot surgeons during operations.

A technician examines DNA in a liquid. The DNA is visible in ultraviolet light as glowing bands of color. Manipulation of DNA, genetic engineering, and gene replacement techniques will be the keys to medicine in the twenty-first century.

▶ FUTURE TREND

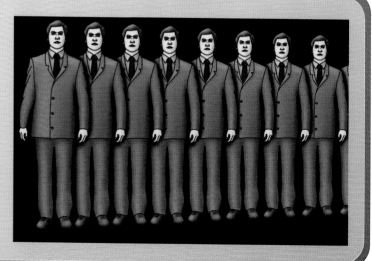

LONG LIFE AND HAPPINESS?
In the future, people will stay strong and healthy for longer than they do today. Transplants and implants will replace worn-out organs. Scientists could add a hundred years to the human life span by finding and replacing the genes that cause aging. So how would you spend your 200th birthday? Perhaps with your cloned children, grandchildren and great-grandchildren? And if they were all identical to you, how would you know which one was the real you?

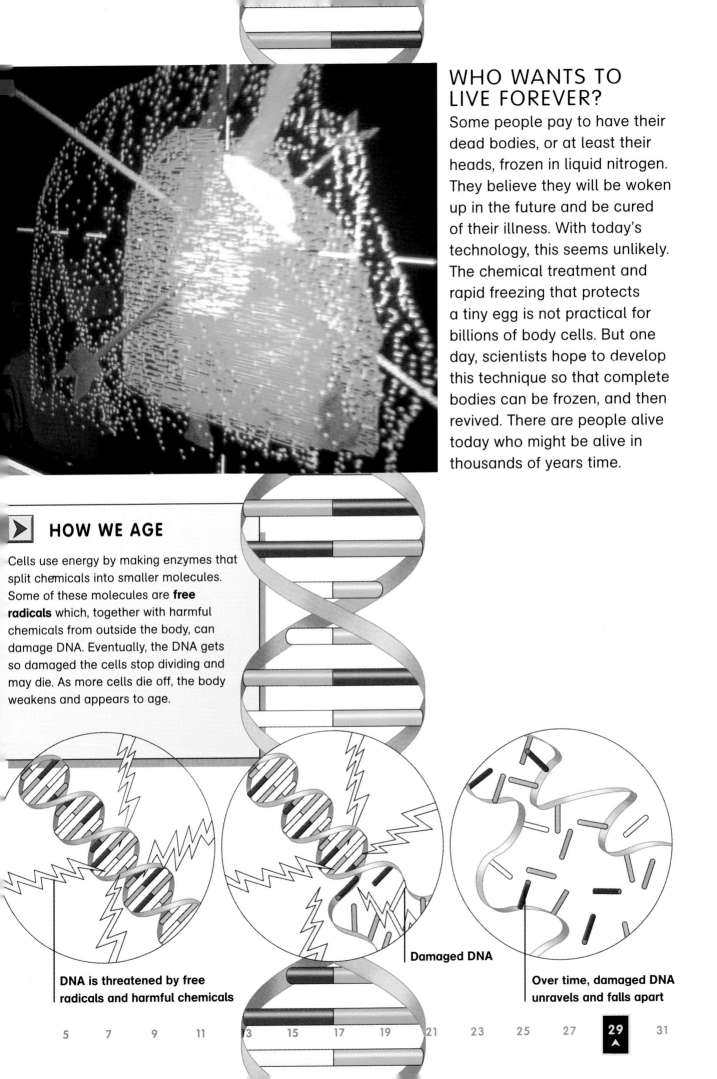

WHO WANTS TO LIVE FOREVER?

Some people pay to have their dead bodies, or at least their heads, frozen in liquid nitrogen. They believe they will be woken up in the future and be cured of their illness. With today's technology, this seems unlikely. The chemical treatment and rapid freezing that protects a tiny egg is not practical for billions of body cells. But one day, scientists hope to develop this technique so that complete bodies can be frozen, and then revived. There are people alive today who might be alive in thousands of years time.

▶ HOW WE AGE

Cells use energy by making enzymes that split chemicals into smaller molecules. Some of these molecules are **free radicals** which, together with harmful chemicals from outside the body, can damage DNA. Eventually, the DNA gets so damaged the cells stop dividing and may die. As more cells die off, the body weakens and appears to age.

DNA is threatened by free radicals and harmful chemicals

Damaged DNA

Over time, damaged DNA unravels and falls apart

GLOSSARY

acupuncture A traditional Chinese technique to reduce pain or treat problems by inserting needles into certain points in the body. This process may activate natural painkilling chemicals in the brain.

anesthetic A drug that causes the body to lose all feeling, including feelings of pain.

antibodies Protein-based chemicals made by white blood cells in response to germs. Some antibodies kill germs; others stick them together. They can be produced artificially by genetically altered bacteria.

arteries Blood vessels that take blood away from the heart. Veins return blood to the heart.

atom The smallest unit that makes up a chemical. Each atom consists of a far smaller nucleus surrounded by specks of fast-moving energy called electrons.

bacteria One-celled living things that split in half to reproduce. In one day, a single bacterium can make 16 million copies of itself.

base pairs Parts of the DNA molecule made up of four types of chemicals (adenine, guanine, cytosine, and thymine) arranged in pairs. Adenine always pairs with thymine, and cytosine with guanine. The sequence of these chemicals on the molecule represents the genetic code that controls how each cell grows.

cell A tiny living unit that makes up your body and every other living thing. It would take well over 2,000 of them just to stretch across your little fingernail.

chiropractic A technique of pulling or pushing the spine and other parts of the body to treat muscular problems and reduce pain.

diabetes A group of conditions caused by a problem of the pancreas (the part of the body that makes insulin), which results in too much sugar in the blood.

diagnosis The identification of a disease by a doctor, usually based on an examination and symptoms.

electromagnet An iron bar surrounded by wire coils, which becomes a powerful magnet when an electric current runs through the wire.

embryo A developing, unborn human baby in the first eight weeks of its life.

enzyme A protein-based chemical made in the body. Each type of enzyme has a particular job to do, such as breaking down food in your intestines.

free radicals These chemicals join easily to other chemicals and can damage DNA inside cells.

gamma ray A ray rather like an x-ray but with more energy. Gamma rays are produced from the nucleus of an atom that is losing energy and falling apart. This type of atom is described as radioactive.

graft In medicine, a graft is a living body part that is transplanted into another part of the body (or another body) where it continues to grow.

hormone A chemical made in the body that controls a particular process. Hormones usually travel around the body in the blood. Lack of a hormone may cause disease.

hypnosis A way of relaxing a person so that they are open to orders or suggestions. Hypnosis can be used to control pain or to overcome deep-seated fears.

immune When the body becomes resistant to (or protected against) a particular disease.

larynx Part of the windpipe in the neck containing the vocal cords which produce sounds for speech. It is often called the voice box.

laser A laser uses an electrical charge to power up atoms and cause them to give out photons—tiny blips of energy that make up light. The photons hit other atoms and make them produce more photons until a powerful, pure beam of light is formed. The rays of light are parallel, making a pencil-like beam.

molecule Two or more atoms joined together.

mutation When a mistake in copying DNA causes a change to the genes. Not all mutations cause disease. Many have no effect on the workings of the cell.

nanorobot A robot that is so tiny that it works on the level of molecules.

nitrogen A gas that makes up 78 percent of the air we breathe. The nitrogen used to freeze living parts is cooled to −285°F. At this temperature, the nitrogen is a liquid rather than a gas.

organ A major part of the body, such as the brain or heart, that does a specific job.

oxygen A gas that makes up 21 percent of the air we breathe. Oxygen is needed by cells to help them break down food chemicals and produce energy. This is why humans need to breathe oxygen to stay alive.

pacemaker An electronic device or implant that delivers tiny electric signals to the heart in order to keep it beating regularly. It is normally placed under the skin of the chest.

paralysis Inability to move. This can be caused by damage to the nerves, brain, or muscles.

polymer A complex chemical often made from a chain of smaller chemicals. Many plastics are polymers.

prescription An order made by a doctor or dentist for a particular drug or medicine. The prescription is sent to a pharmacist, who provides the drug.

proteins A huge range of complicated chemicals that fulfill vital jobs in the body. Proteins are made up of long chains of smaller molecules called amino acids.

protozoa A group of one-celled living things. Protozoa that cause disease include the types responsible for malaria—a fatal disease spread by mosquitoes that affects 200 million people worldwide.

silicon chip A tiny electrical circuit made from a piece of silicon crystal, found in most electronic machines, including televisions. Also called a microchip.

sperm Cells made by male animals for breeding. The sperm cell swims by beating its long tail. The head of the sperm cell contains DNA.

stone In medicine, a stonelike object that can form in the gall bladder next to the liver, in the kidneys, or elsewhere in the body. Stones are formed from chemicals in these organs that turn into crystals. They can become painful if they get too big.

symptom A change in the body that is noticed by the patient and may be triggered by a disease. A high temperature is often a symptom of an infection.

tooth decay A hole in the tough, outer layer of a tooth caused by acid made by germs. If the hole reaches the tooth's sensitive center, it can cause toothache.

transfusion A transfer of blood into the body from a donor to a patient.

transplant A living part of a body (from another human or an animal) placed in the body of a patient.

vibrations What happens when an object is physically shaking.

virus A tiny living thing that causes diseases. A virus consists of a central core of genetic material surrounded by a protein shell. Diseases caused by viruses include chickenpox and yellow fever.

x-ray A ray similar to a light or radio wave but with a far higher energy level. X-rays are soaked up by solid materials, such as bone. This makes the bones show up clearly in an x-ray photograph.

zero gravity This describes conditions in outer space, where the force of gravity that pulls us all down to Earth does not operate. An astronaut in space feels weightless.

INDEX